Weather

Lynn Huggins-Cooper

Illustrated by
Shelagh McNicholas
David Burroughs

W
FRANKLIN WATTS
LONDON • SYDNEY

About the author
Lynn Huggins-Cooper is a lecturer in primary science at Newcastle University and specialises in interactive teaching methods. She also creates wildlife gardens for schools and runs a conservation club.

This edition 2008
Published by Franklin Watts
338 Euston Road, London NW1 3BH

Franklin Watts Australia
Level 17/207 Kent Street, Sydney NSW 2000

Series editor: Rachel Cooke
Art director: Jonathan Hair
Design: James Marks

A CIP catalogue record for this book is available from the British Library.

ISBN 978 0 7496 7867 8
Printed in China

Franklin Watts is a division of Hachette Children's Books, an Hachette Livre UK company.

Contents

Joe likes to play outside – whatever the weather. Come and join him!

What's the weather like?

Every day when Joe gets up, he looks out of the window. What's the weather going to be like today?

Here are some different kinds of weather:

Rainy

Sunny

Windy

Snowy

What's the weather like today where you are?

It's a warm, sunny day. Joe and his mum are going on a picnic! What will Joe choose to wear?

When it's hot, we wear clothes that help us to keep cool, like shorts and T-shirts.

When it's cold, we wear warm jumpers and jackets.

Is it always warm when it's sunny? Would you wear shorts and T-shirts on a sunny day in winter?

7

Joe enjoys his picnic. He thinks his dark glasses and hat look funny!

How is Joe protected from the sun?

The **sun** gives us heat. We have to be careful, though - the sun can burn our skin and make it red and sore. These things protect us from sunburn:

Sun hats

Sun block

Loose T-shirt with sleeves

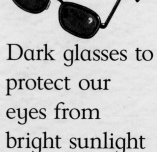

Dark glasses to protect our eyes from bright sunlight

During the day, the sun gives us light. If something blocks the sunlight, it casts shadows.

At night, when the sun sets, it gets dark. We use electric lights to see by.

Mum sits under the tree. She likes it because it is cool and shady.

Never look straight at the sun - even with dark glasses on! The bright light can hurt your eyes.

Kite weather!

The wind has started to blow. Joe and his mum are flying a kite. The wind carries it high in the air!

How can Joe tell which way the wind is blowing?

Wind is moving air.

Cold winds blow from cold places - like the snowy **Poles**.

Hot winds blow from hot places - like a baking **desert**.

The wind has brought some clouds. Joe likes spotting animal shapes in them.

Clouds are made from tiny water droplets in the air.

Sometimes, water falls from the clouds as **rain**.

Rain water collects in rivers, lakes and the sea. Some of it rises up into the air again as an invisible gas. High in the sky, the gas turns back into water droplets.

? ? ?

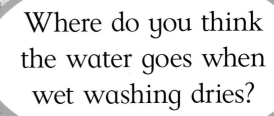

Where do you think the water goes when wet washing dries?

It's raining

Now the clouds have hidden the sun. It looks grey and dark. Soon it starts to rain.

Inside the clouds, water droplets join together.

The drops get too big and heavy and fall out of the sky - as rain!

Joe loves jumping in puddles. What clothes would he need for a walk in the rain?

12

Joe and Mum have found somewhere to shelter. The sun is trying to come out again!

Look, Mum! A rainbow!

Rainbows happen when sunlight shines through raindrops. The white sunlight breaks up into different colours - and we see a rainbow!

We see seven colours in rainbows.

red

orange

yellow 2

green 3

blue 4

indigo 5

violet 6

Making plants grow

Joe and Mum go home. The rain has stopped. Water droplets glitter everywhere. The plants won't need watering tonight!

My tomatoes are coming along nicely.

These apples look ripe.

Plants need light and water to grow properly.

Plants grow all year round - but different things grow in different **seasons**.

In autumn, the leaves turn brown and blow away.

As summer ends, the fruit is ripe and ready to eat.

Are there any fruits or vegetables that you eat in the summer but not in the winter?

In winter the apple tree's branches are bare.

The fruit grows larger through the warm summer.

The blossom petals drop off, leaving behind tiny fruit.

In spring, the tree blossoms and its leaves unfurl.

15

Stormy weather

Joe's playing indoors today. A storm rages outside. Thunder rumbles and lightning flashes.

You get very strong winds in a **storm**. Use the pictures to see how windy it is outside today!

Calm: the trees are still.

Gentle breeze: leaves rustle.

Fresh breeze: branches sway and leaves blow about.

Storms can be dangerous, but Joe knows he is safe indoors. Cleo, his cat, is not so sure!

The storm will go away soon, Cleo.

Stay safe in a thunderstorm - inside a house or in a car.

Don't shelter under a tree because **lightning** could strike it.

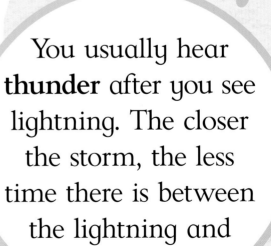

You usually hear **thunder** after you see lightning. The closer the storm, the less time there is between the lightning and the thunder.

Gale: twigs and branches may break off trees.

Hurricane: very strong wind which can blow down trees and houses!

Hail!

The storm is getting noisy now! Joe listens to hail drumming on the roof.

Water falls to the ground in lots of different ways.

Sometimes it 'spits' - and only a few drops fall.

Sometimes it drizzles. The rain drops are tiny and light.

Sometimes it pours with rain.

Sometimes, in stormy weather, it **hails**. Water droplets freeze suddenly high in the sky. They fall to the ground as chunks of **ice** or hailstones.

Mum has collected some hailstones in a dish. They look like little white peas!

Sometimes, in cold winter weather, it **snows**.

In some parts of the world, hailstones can be huge - and dangerous! In really bad storms, they can be bigger than tennis balls.

Snow is made in the clouds when water droplets freeze around a tiny piece of dust.

If you look at snowflakes with a magnifier, you see many different and beautiful shapes. But they all have six sides or points!

Snow and ice

Joe and Mum are talking about the snow last winter. They remember how Joe built a snowcat.

Snow only falls when it is cold. We usually see snow during the winter.

Some mountains are so high that they are always cold and always covered in snow and ice.

Joe loves snow!
He likes to lie down and flap his arms and legs in it. When he gets up, he's made a 'snow angel'!

When it's very cold, snowflakes are small and powdery. When it's a little warmer, the flakes are larger - like fluffy white feathers!

21

Joe and Mum also remember one day when it was cold and frosty. Everything was white and glittered in the sunshine.

Frost happens after clear, cold nights. Water droplets on the ground, on plants and on spiders' webs freeze into ice.

If it stays cold for a while, long needles of frost are made. This is called hoar frost.

Have you ever woken up and seen the grass covered in frost? What do you remember about it?

Ice is frozen water. It is solid, and cannot flow.

Icicles form where dripping water freezes.

When it gets warmer, the ice begins to melt and the icicles drip slowly away.

Icicles hung from the roof, and the pond was frozen solid. Joe was careful not to slip over on the path.

Water changes to ice when it gets cold. What happens when water is heated? Look back at page 11 for a clue.

Weather watch

The storm is over at last. Joe has made his own weather station. Mum is helping him collect information.

Scientists collect all sorts of information to study the weather. They try to discover what the weather will be like tomorrow or further in the future.

They measure how much rain falls.

What is Joe doing to watch the weather?

They measure
the temperature
- how hot it is.

They use **satellites**
in space to see how
clouds and air are
moving around our planet.

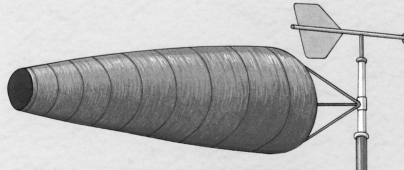

They check the
strength of the wind
and where it is
coming from.

We see their results when
we watch the **weather
forecast** on television.

All sorts of weather

Joe enjoys all sorts
of weather!

Hail

Rain

???

What season
do you think each
photo is showing? How
can you tell?

Snow

26

Frost and ice

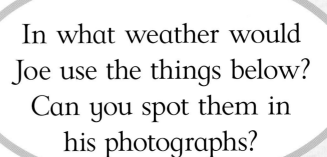

In what weather would Joe use the things below? Can you spot them in his photographs?

Fog

Sunshine

Wind

kite

ice skates

woolly gloves, hat and scarf

torch

Wellington boots

brolly

sun hat

Try this yourself!

Have some weather fun!

Weather watching

Today, there are lots of scientific ways of forecasting the weather. In the past, people used seaweed and pinecones to decide if rain was on the way. Find a pinecone or some seaweed and try it for yourself.

If the spines on the pinecone are closed, it means the air is damp - and it may rain. If the spines are open, the air is dry and it will be a fine day!

If the seaweed feels dry and crispy, it will be a dry, sunny day.

If the seaweed feels rubbery, it might rain!

Cloud gazing

On a day when the clouds are broken up and fluffy, try Joe's game of spotting shapes in them (see page 11). Now paint a picture using the cloud shape as a starting point.

The right kit

The clothes these people are wearing are just right for the weather in their part of the world.

Why do you think this woman's outfit is good for the cold Poles?

Why do you think this man's outfit is good in the hot desert?

Design your own outfits for different kinds of weather - one for hot weather and one for cold weather.

Useful words

cloud: Water droplets massed together in the air.

desert: A very dry place where few plants grow.

fog: A kind of cloud that forms close to the ground.

frost: When water on the surface of things such as plants freezes.

hail: Chunks of ice that sometimes fall in a storm.

ice: Frozen water.

lightning: Electric flashes made by some storms.

Poles: The far north and south of the Earth where it is always cold and icy.

rain: Water that falls from clouds.

satellite: A machine sent into space to circle and watch the Earth.

seasons: The different times of year - spring, summer, autumn and winter - with their own types of weather.

snow: The frozen flakes of ice that fall in cold weather.

storm: Very windy and often very wet weather.

sun: Our nearest star that gives us heat and light.

thunder: The noise made when lightning flashes.

weather forecast: Saying what the weather will be like in the future.

weather station: A place where information about the weather is collected.

wind: Moving air.

About this book

This book encourages children to explore and discover science in their local, familiar environment - in the garden or at the park. By starting from 'where they are', it aims to increase children's knowledge and understanding of the world around them, encouraging them to examine the natural world and its processes closely and from a more scientific perspective.

The weather is explored, focusing on its daily changes and linking it to the seasons. Questions are asked to build on children's natural curiosity and encourage them to think about what they are reading. Some questions send children back to the book to find the answers, others point to new ideas that, through discussion, the readers may 'discover' for themselves.

Index